THE OFFICIAL CELTIC ANNUAL 2019

Written by Joe Sullivan
Designed by Chris Dalrymple

A Grange Publication

© 2018. Published by Grange Communications Ltd., Edinburgh, under licence from Celtic Football Club. Printed in the EU.

Photographs by Alan Whyte and Ryan Whyte, Angus Johnston, Celtic Multi-Media.

ISBN 978-1-912595-03-7

CONTENTS

L CLUB

BRENDAN RODGERS

TO say that Brendan Rodgers has made a success of his first two seasons as manager at Celtic Park would truly be an understatement.

A year after the Irishman's arrival at Celtic Park was hailed by thousands inside the ground, he stood on the same hallowed turf with the treble of the League Cup, the Scottish Cup and the SPFL trophy shimmering in the Paradise sun.

Not only had a sixth successive title been won for the third time in the club's history, not only had the club's fourth treble been won – but he had led the Celts to an Invincible Treble with not a single game being lost as the Hoops marched to the three trophies over the course of the campaign.

What could he do to get anywhere near that success the following season? What could he do to equal that success? What could he do to surpass that success? The answer was a simple one, even if the execution and implementation of getting there would obviously be very difficult indeed.

He had to win an unprecedented Double Treble – and that's exactly what he did.

Brendan Rodgers' first trophy success at Celtic, the League Cup win over Aberdeen in 2016, proved to be the club's 100th top-level trophy and when he lifted the same trophy a year later with a 2-0 win over Motherwell, he became the first manager in the club's history to win the first four trophies available – even eclipsing the great Jock Stein.

That he was able to go on and add No.5 and No.6 to that achievement is nothing short of miraculous considering the tough season Celtic had gone through.

The title was next to arrive as a resounding 5-0 victory over Rangers delivered an amazing seven-in-a-row for only the second time in the club's history.

Following the presentation of the trophy, there was the small matter of the Scottish Cup final

CLUB HONOURS

SCOTTISH LEAGUE WINNERS [49 TIMES]
1892/93, 1893/94, 1895/96, 1897/98, 1904/05, 1905/06, 1906/07, 1907/08, 1908/09, 1909/10, 1913/14, 1914/15, 1915/16, 1916/17, 1918/19, 1921/22, 1925/26, 1935/36, 1937/38, 1953/54, 1965/66, 1966/67, 1967/68, 1968/69, 1969/70, 1970/71, 1971/72, 1972/73, 1973/74, 1976/77, 1978/79, 1980/81, 1981/82, 1985/86, 1987/88, 1997/98, 2000/01, 2001/02, 2003/04, 2005/06, 2006/07, 2007/08, 2011/12, 2012/13, 2013/14, 2014/15, 2015/16, 2016/17, 2017/18

SCOTTISH CUP WINNERS [38 TIMES]
1892, 1899, 1900, 1904, 1907, 1908, 1911, 1912, 1914, 1923, 1925, 1927, 1931, 1933, 1937, 1951, 1954, 1965, 1967, 1969, 1971, 1972, 1974, 1975, 1977, 1980, 1985, 1988, 1989, 1995, 2001, 2004, 2005, 2007, 2011, 2013, 2017, 2018

LEAGUE CUP WINNERS [17 TIMES]
1956/57, 1957/58, 1965/66, 1966/67, 1967/68, 1968/69, 1969/70, 1974/75,1982/83, 1997/98, 1999/00, 2000/01, 2005/06, 2008/09, 2014/15, 2016/17, 2017/18

EUROPEAN CUP WINNERS 1967
CORONATION CUP WINNERS 1953

to ensure that, for the first time in the history of Scottish football, the second successive treble was on.

Once more, Brendan Rodgers' Celts delivered and the unique Double Treble trophies arrived at Paradise to a tumultuous reception in an open-top bus following another Hampden win.

And, once more Brendan Rodgers stood on the same hallowed turf with the treble of the League Cup, the Scottish Cup and the SPFL trophy shimmering in the Paradise sun.

MANAGER FACTFILE

D.O.B: 26/01/73 BORN: CARNLOUGH, IRELAND

PLAYING CAREER RECORD:

BALLYMENA UNITED (1987-90) READING (1990-93)
NEWPORT (1993-94) WITNEY TOWN (1994-95)
NEWBURY TOWN (1995-96)

AS MANAGER:

WATFORD (2008-09) READING (2009)
SWANSEA CITY (2010-12) LIVERPOOL (2012-15)
CELTIC (2016 TO DATE)

MANAGERIAL HONOURS:

LEAGUE CHAMPIONS (2016/17, 2017/18)
SCOTTISH CUP WINNERS (2016/17, 2017/18)
LEAGUE CUP WINNERS (2016/17, 2017/18)

THE CELTIC PARK GOAL MAZE

BRENDAN Rodgers' Celtic side are famed for playing the ball out from the back and many goals have been scored following an array of passing between the Hoops from one end of the ground to the other. Can you find the route the ball made from one goal to the other?

Find out how the goal was scored on page 62.

SPOT THE DIFFERENCE

THERE are 10 differences between these post-match team shots taken after Scott Brown's testimonial match at the end of last season. The first one has been circled, but can you spot the rest?

Answers on page 62.

DOUBLE TREBLE WINNERS

2016/17   2017/18

JULY

JUST three weeks after securing the domestic treble as Invincibles, Celtic's first-team squad reported back for pre-season training ahead of their UEFA Champions League qualification campaign, which would begin in mid-July with a tie against Irish side, Linfield.

Following a training camp in Austria and several pre-season games, Brendan Rodgers' side headed to Belfast for the first leg of their second qualifying round.

And they recorded a comfortable 2-0 victory, courtesy of goals from Mark Haughey, who touched the ball into his own net under pressure from Scott Sinclair, and Tom Rogic. Both Celts were also on the scoresheet in the return leg at Celtic Park, as the Hoops ran out 4-0 winners on the night for a 6-0 aggregate victory.

JULY FIXTURES (HOME FIXTURES IN BOLD)

14	UCL	2-0	v Linfield	(Haughey og, Rogic)
19	**UCL**	**4-0**	**v Linfield**	**(Sinclair 2, Armstrong, Rogic)**
26	UCL	0-0	v Rosenborg	

Sinclair netted a double that night, while Stuart Armstrong also got in on the scoring act.

The reward was a tie against Norwegian champions, Rosenborg, in the third qualifying round of the Champions League, and the first leg saw the sides fight out a goal-less draw, ensuring a tricky away tie in Trondheim at the beginning of August to see who would progress to the play-off round.

AUGUST

BRENDAN Rodgers' side produced a superb away European performance to beat Rosenborg 1-0 and take a step closer to the group stages of the UEFA Champions League.

The Hoops were disciplined and dominant and got their reward through James Forrest, who fired home the only goal of the tie.

The following weekend, Celtic launched the defence of their Premiership title with a 4-1 home win over Hearts, with Leigh Griffiths netting a double in the demolition of the Edinburgh team.

That win was quickly followed by an even more emphatic victory, this time in the League Cup, with the Hoops hitting five without reply against Kilmarnock. Kieran Tierney was captain for the night, and he crowned a stunning performance with a blistering 40-yard strike that was the pick of Celtic's five goals.

AUGUST FIXTURES (HOME FIXTURES IN BOLD)

2	UCL	1-0	v Rosenborg	(Forrest)
5	**SPFL**	**4-1**	**v Hearts**	**(Griffiths 2, Sinclair, McGregor)**
8	**LC**	**5-0**	**v Kilmarnock**	**(Griffiths 2, Ralston, Tierney, Armstrong)**
11	SPFL	1-0	v Partick Thistle	(Ntcham)
16	**UCL**	**5-0**	**v Astana**	**(Sinclair 2, Forrest, own goals 2)**
19	SPFL	2-0	v Kilmarnock	(McGregor, Forrest)
22	UCL	3-4	v Astana	(Sinclair, Ntcham, Griffiths)
26	**SPFL**	**1-1**	**v St Johnstone**	**(McGregor)**

THE TOP 3

	P	W	D	L	F	A	GD	PTS
Aberdeen	4	4	0	0	10	5	5	12
Celtic	**4**	**3**	**1**	**0**	**8**	**2**	**6**	**10**
St Johnstone	4	3	1	0	8	3	5	10

Olivier Ntcham scored his first goal for Celtic in the 1-0 Glasgow derby win over Partick Thistle at Firhill before the Hoops faced FC Astana of Kazakhstan in the first leg of their UEFA Champions League play off tie.

And on the night, the Hoops produced a performance which had Paradise rocking, scoring five goals without reply and effectively ensuring group-stage football for the second consecutive season.

Scott Sinclair, with a double, and James Forrest were among the scorers, while Astana chipped in with two own goals. The return leg saw the Kazakhstan side win 4-3 on the night, but the Hoops triumphed 8-4 on aggregate, and Champions League football was back at Celtic Park again.

Having also beaten Kilmarnock 2-0 at Rugby Park in August, the Hoops ended the month with a 1-1 draw against St Johnstone, with Callum McGregor supplying Celtic's equaliser.

SEPTEMBER

CELTIC played seven games across three competitions in September, winning five of those games and losing just one.

That solitary loss was against Paris Saint-Germain in the opening group-stage game of the Champions League, with the French side winning 5-0 at Paradise. However, Brendan Rodgers' side also recorded an impressive 3-0 away European win against Anderlecht in Belgium, courtesy of goals from Leigh Griffiths, Patrick Roberts and Scott Sinclair.

The month had started with a 4-1 win over Hamilton Accies at New Douglas Park, with Scott Sinclair netting a double and Stuart Armstrong also on the scoresheet. And there was a debut goal for on-loan French striker, Odsonne Edouard.

SEPTEMBER FIXTURES (HOME FIXTURES IN BOLD)

8	SPFL	4-1	v Hamilton Accies	(Sinclair 2, Armstrong, Edouard)
12	**UCL**	**0-5**	**v Paris Saint-Germain**	
16	**SPFL**	**4-0**	**v Ross County**	**(Forrest 2, Rogic, Dembele)**
20	LC	4-0	v Dundee	(Forrest 2, Sinclair, McGregor)
23	SPFL	2-0	v Rangers	(Rogic, Griffiths)
27	UCL	3-0	v Anderlecht	(Griffiths, Roberts, Sinclair)
30	**SPFL**	**2-2**	**v Hibernian**	**(McGregor 2)**

THE TOP 3

	P	W	D	L	F	A	GD	PTS
Celtic	**8**	**6**	**2**	**0**	**20**	**5**	**15**	**20**
Aberdeen	8	6	2	0	15	6	9	20
St Johnstone	8	4	2	2	17	11	6	14

A 4-0 League Cup win over Dundee at Dens Park put the Hoops into the semi-final of the competition before they travelled to Ibrox for their first meeting of the season with Rangers.

Once again, Brendan Rodgers' side dominated the fixture and two second-half goals from Tom Rogic and Leigh Griffiths gave the Hoops all three points.

The month ended with a tricky home game against Hibernian at Celtic Park, and the visitors came from behind to lead 2-1 with 13 minutes of the match remaining, courtesy of two John McGinn goals.

However, Callum McGregor scored his second of the game to level the score at 2-2 and ensure a share of the spoils.

2016/17

2017/18

OCTOBER

OLIVIER Ntcham was the match winner for Celtic in their home game against Dundee, the French midfielder scoring the only goal of the game to give the Hoops all three points.

It was the start of a busy week for Brendan Rodgers' side, who travelled to Germany to take on Bayern Munich in the Champions League. And it was the Germans who took all three points with a 3-0 victory in the Allianz Arena.

Celtic didn't have much time to dwell on the result, however, as less than three days later they faced Hibernian at Hampden in the League Cup semi-final. The sides produced a six-goal thriller in the National Stadium, with the cup holders coming out on top, winning 4-2 thanks to a double each from Mikael Lustig and Moussa Dembele.

OCTOBER FIXTURES (HOME FIXTURES IN BOLD)

14	SPFL	1-0	v Dundee	(Ntcham)
18	UCL	0-3	v Bayern Munich	
21	LC	4-2	v Hibernian	(Lustig 2, Dembele 2)
25	SPFL	3-0	v Aberdeen	(Tierney, Dembele 2)
28	**SPFL**	**1-1**	**v Kilmarnock**	**(Griffiths)**
31	**UCL**	**1-2**	**v Bayern Munich**	**(McGregor)**

THE TOP 3

	P	W	D	L	F	A	GD	PTS
Celtic	**11**	**8**	**3**	**0**	**25**	**6**	**19**	**27**
Aberdeen	11	8	2	1	18	10	8	26
St Johnstone	11	6	3	2	24	13	11	21

The following Wednesday, Celtic travelled to Pittodrie and produced a stunning performance to beat Aberdeen 3-0. Kieran Tierney opened the scoring with a blistering effort from a tight angle inside the box, and a double from Dembele confirmed Celtic's superiority.

Frustration was on the cards that weekend, however, as Celtic had to be content with a point in a 1-1 home draw against Kilmarnock, Leigh Griffiths scoring for the Celts.

The run of October fixtures finished on Hallowe'en with a home game against Bayern Munich. Despite the 2-1 defeat, the Hoops played superbly well on the night, with Callum McGregor drawing them level late in the second-half before the Germans snatched a late winner for a victory they barely deserved.

DOUBLE TREBLE WINNERS

2016/17   2017/18

NOVEMBER

CELTIC didn't play a single game at home in the month of November, yet they still managed to ensure that the League Cup remained in the Paradise trophy room.

A 4-0 victory over St Johnstone at McDiarmid Park kicked off the month, and it was a historic victory as the win extended the unbeaten domestic run to 63 games, beating the previous record of 62 games set by Willie Maley's Celtic side between 1915 and 1917.

NOVEMBER FIXTURES (HOME FIXTURES IN BOLD)

4	SPFL	**4-0**	v St Johnstone	(Sinclair, Dembele, Ntcham, own goal)
18	SPFL	1-0	v Ross County	(Griffiths)
22	UCL	1-7	v Paris Saint-Germain	(Dembele)
26	LC	**2-0**	v Motherwell	(Forrest, Dembele)
29	SPFL	1-1	v Motherwell	(Sinclair)

THE TOP 3

	P	W	D	L	F	A	GD	PTS
Celtic	**14**	**10**	**4**	**0**	**32**	**7**	**24**	**34**
Aberdeen	15	9	3	3	23	18	5	30
Rangers	15	8	3	4	31	17	14	27

And the Hoops followed that up with a 1-0 win over Ross County at Dingwall, the only goal of the game coming courtesy of a stunning Leigh Griffiths' free kick late in the game.

Celtic then took on Paris Saint-Germain in the Parc des Princes, and the Hoops were ahead inside the first minute of the game through Moussa Dembele.

It was the first goal PSG had conceded in this season's competition. Unfortunately, they went on to score seven goals of their own to take all three points.

If the Celtic squad were nursing any wounds from that heavy defeat, they didn't show it at Hampden the following Sunday as they defeated Motherwell 2-0 in the League Cup final to retain the trophy.

James Forrest gave Celtic the lead early in the second half and Moussa Dembele converted a penalty to guarantee victory.

The following Wednesday the sides met again, this time at Fir Park, and it took a late Scott Sinclair goal to equalise for the Hoops after a Mikael Lustig own goal had given the home side the lead.

DOUBLE TREBLE WINNERS

DECEMBER

THE month of December began with a convincing 5-1 victory over Motherwell at Celtic Park – the third game between the sides in six days – with Odsonne Edouard producing an impressive hat-trick.

And though the next game was a 1-0 defeat at home to Anderlecht, Brendan Rodgers' side still progressed to the last 32 of the UEFA Europa League, ensuring European football after Christmas.

For the second time in the season, the Hoops then fought out a 2-2 draw with Hibernian, though it was a game they could and should have won.

Scott Sinclair gave Celtic a two-goal lead, and the Hoops were in control of the game before Hibs grabbed two goals in three minutes to draw level. And it took a Mikael Lustig goal-line clearance to prevent the unbeaten run being ended, though Celtic then went up the park and nearly scored a last-gasp winner themselves.

A 3-1 win at home to Hamilton in the midweek was followed by another trip to Scotland's capital, this time to take on Hearts at Tynecastle.

And on the day, it was the home side who were deserved winners, though the 4-0 scoreline was one that would have surprised many observers.

DECEMBER FIXTURES (HOME FIXTURES IN BOLD)

2	**SPFL**	**5-1**	**v Motherwell**	**(Edouard 3, Forrest 2)**
5	**UCL**	**0-1**	**v Anderlecht**	
10	SPFL	2-2	v Hibernian	(Sinclair 2)
13	**SPFL**	**3-1**	**v Hamilton Accies**	**(Ntcham, Forrest, Sinclair)**
17	SPFL	0-4	v Hearts	
20	**SPFL**	**2-0**	**v Partick Thistle**	**(Tierney, Armstrong)**
23	**SPFL**	**3-0**	**v Aberdeen**	**(Lustig, Ntcham, Hayes)**
26	SPFL	2-0	v Dundee	(Forrest, Griffiths)
30	**SPFL**	**0-0**	**v Rangers**	

THE TOP 3

	P	W	D	L	F	A	GD	PTS
Celtic	**22**	**15**	**6**	**1**	**48**	**15**	**33**	**51**
Aberdeen	22	13	4	5	33	24	9	43
Rangers	22	12	4	6	41	25	16	40

It brought to an end Celtic's historic unbeaten run, and though there was disappointment at the defeat, the Celtic fans at Tynecastle stood at the end of the game to applaud the incredible efforts of the team in going 69 domestic games unbeaten, winning 60 of those fixtures and scoring 197 goals in the process.

Normal service was resumed then, however, with three consecutive wins and three clean sheets too. A 2-0 derby win over Partick Thistle was followed by a top-of-the-table clash at home to Aberdeen, with Brendan Rodgers' side winning 3-0. And on Boxing Day, the Hoops won 2-0 against Dundee at Dens Park.

The Scottish champions faced the final fixture of 2017 – a Glasgow derby at Paradise against Rangers – but signed off with a 0-0 draw.

JANUARY

THE winter break took up almost the first three weeks of the year before a flurry of games – and wins – in a 10-day period.

The first game of the return featured a Scottish Cup match and the visit of Championship side Brechin City who had experienced only one win all season – in the previous round of the cup when they beat Highland League side Buckie Thistle 3-2 with a late goal.

Their cup luck ran out pretty quickly against the Celts with James Forrest scoring after only two minutes and a 2-0 half-time lead was increased to 5-0 by the end of the game.

Celtic's next couple of games weren't so cut and dried as both featured tight scorelines but the Hoops still carried on their winning ways.

First up was a trip to Firhill to play Partick Thistle and the Maryhill side took a first-half lead from the spot before Scott Sinclair equalised, also from 12 yards, and then a clever Leigh Griffiths' goal gave the Celts full points.

JANUARY FIXTURES (HOME FIXTURES IN BOLD)

20	**SC**	**5-0**	**v Brechin City**	**(Forrest, Sinclair, Ntcham, Boyata, Edouard)**
23	SPFL	2-1	v Partick Thistle	(Sinclair, Griffiths)
27	**SPFL**	**1-0**	**v Hibernian**	**(Griffiths)**
30	SPFL	3-1	v Hearts	(Edouard, Boyata, Dembele)

THE TOP 3

	P	W	D	L	F	A	GD	PTS
Celtic	**25**	**18**	**6**	**1**	**54**	**17**	**37**	**60**
Aberdeen	25	15	4	6	40	29	11	49
Rangers	24	14	4	6	45	26	19	46

Griffiths was on hand again four days later when he was the difference between the Celts and his former club as the Hoops beat Hibernian 1-0 at Celtic Park.

Just three days later, the other half of the Edinburgh pairing visited the East End of Glasgow but the scoreline was much more convincing as the Celts were 3-0 up by the 36th minute with the game finishing 3-1.

FEBRUARY

EXPERIENCING domestic defeat, thankfully, has been a rare occurrence over the past two seasons and only the second such loss came in the opening game of February when a 70th-minute goal from Youssouf Mulumbu gave Kilmarnock the spoils at Rugby Park.

In the very next game, though, James Forrest added to his already sparkling season by notching his very first hat-trick as Celtic welcomed Partick Thistle in the Scottish Cup and, although the visitors made it 3-2 just six minutes from the end, the Hoops saw out the contest to book their place in the next round.

The Bhoys then returned to continental competition as they hosted Zenit St Petersburg in the first-leg of their Europa League last-32 clash. Callum McGregor's fantastic finish gave the Hoops a well-deserved 1-0 win on the night but in the return match in Russia seven days later, Brendan Rodgers' side went down 3-0, bringing an end to their European adventure for the season.

FEBRUARY FIXTURES (HOME FIXTURES IN BOLD)

3	SPFL	0-1	v Kilmarnock	
10	**SC**	**3-2**	**v Partick Thistle**	**(Forrest 3)**
15	**UEL**	**1-0**	**v Zenit St Petersburg**	**(McGregor)**
18	**SPFL**	**0-0**	**v St Johnstone**	
22	UEL	0-3	Zenit St Petersburg	
25	SPFL	2-0	v Aberdeen	(Dembele, Tierney)

THE TOP 3

	P	W	D	L	F	A	GD	PTS
Celtic	**28**	**19**	**7**	**2**	**56**	**18**	**38**	**64**
Rangers	29	18	4	7	59	32	27	58
Aberdeen	28	16	4	8	43	33	10	52

In between the ties with Zenit, the Celts were held to a goal-less draw by St Johnstone, though they still increased their lead at the top of the table to nine points. And they preserved their commanding advantage at the league summit with an excellent win away to Aberdeen towards the end of the month.

Moussa Dembele headed the Hoops into a first-half lead and, despite being reduced to 10 men when Mikael Lustig picked up a second booking, Kieran Tierney's rasping strike in the closing stages sealed a priceless three points in the title race.

2016/17   2017/18

MARCH

HAVING cemented their position at the top of the table, Celtic were back on Scottish Cup duty at the start of March as they took on Morton in Paradise. The Championship side kept the hosts at bay in the first half but their resistance crumbled after the interval as a double from Moussa Dembele, including one from the penalty spot, and a late effort from Odsonne Edouard sealed the Hoops' spot in the semi-finals of the competition.

The next weekend saw the champions head to Ibrox for the third meeting of the season with Rangers. In a pulsating clash, Tom Rogic and Dembele twice cancelled out goals from Josh Windass and Daniel Candeias in the first half, leaving the match evenly poised at the interval. A straight red card for Jozo Simunovic early in the second period looked to have handed the initiative to the home side, but the 10 men rallied superbly and substitute Edouard's wonderful winner saw the Bhoys claim the spoils.

MARCH FIXTURES (HOME FIXTURES IN BOLD)

3	SC	3-0	**v Morton**	**(Dembele 2 (1 pen), Edouard)**
11	SPFL	3-2	v Rangers	(Rogic, Dembele, Edouard)
18	SPFL	0-0	v Motherwell	
31	SPFL	3-0	**v Ross County**	**(Dembele, Armstrong, Rogic)**

THE TOP 3

	P	W	D	L	F	A	GD	PTS
Celtic	**31**	**21**	**8**	**2**	**62**	**20**	**42**	**71**
Rangers	32	18	5	9	63	38	25	59
Aberdeen	31	18	5	8	48	34	14	59

Brendan Rodgers' men were unable to follow that thrilling victory with another three points, with a resilient Motherwell holding them to a goal-less stalemate at Fir Park. But, following the international break, they returned to winning ways, comfortably dispatching Ross County 3-0 thanks to goals from Dembele, Stuart Armstrong and Rogic to keep them well clear of their title rivals.

DOUBLE TREBLE WINNERS

APRIL

CELTIC were in midweek action at the start of the month as they contested their rearranged fixture with Dundee, which had been postponed at the end of February due to the 'Beast from the East'. There would be no blizzard of goals on a frustrating evening in Paradise, however, as a dogged Dens Park side held the Hoops to a goal-less draw.

Nonetheless, the share of the spoils did stretch the champions' lead at the top of the table, and by the end of the week they had moved within one victory of the title after defeating Hamilton Accies 2-1 at New Douglas Park. It looked as though it would be a routine victory for the visitors after Callum McGregor fired them into an early lead with a crisp shot inside the box, but Rakish Bingham levelled for the Lanarkshire side. Either side of half-time, the match swung decisively in Celtic's direction. Three minutes before the break, Darren Lyon earned his marching orders for the hosts and within a minute of the restart, Leigh Griffiths nodded home the winner from Scott Sinclair's delivery.

APRIL FIXTURES (HOME FIXTURES IN BOLD)

4	SPFL	0-0	v Dundee	
8	SPFL	2-1	v Hamilton	(McGregor, Griffiths)
15	SC	4-0	v Rangers	(Rogic, McGregor, Dembele (pen), Ntcham (pen))
21	SPFL	1-2	v Hibernian	(Edouard)
29	**SPFL**	**5-0**	**v Rangers**	**(Edouard 2, Forrest, Rogic, McGregor)**

THE TOP 3

	P	W	D	L	F	A	GD	PTS
Celtic	**35**	**23**	**9**	**3**	**70**	**23**	**47**	**78**
Aberdeen	35	21	5	9	54	36	18	68
Rangers	35	20	5	10	69	44	25	65

The Bhoys then turned their attentions to the Scottish Cup as they crossed swords again with Rangers at Hampden. In a completely one-sided semi-final, the champions swept aside their city rivals 4-0. Fine finishes from Tom Rogic and McGregor had the holders in charge at the interval and Moussa Dembele and Olivier Ntcham converted from the penalty spot in the second half to book a meeting with Motherwell in the showpiece on May 19.

That left Brendan Rodgers' side free to focus on wrapping up the title. They failed in their first opportunity to cross the finishing line, going down to a 2-1 defeat away to Hibernian, with Odsonne Edouard on target.

But they more than made up for that result the following weekend as they sealed seven-in-a-row in scintillating style, trouncing Rangers 5-0 at Celtic Park. The outstanding Edouard bagged a brilliant brace, with James Forrest, Rogic and McGregor also on target as the champions ran riot against their city rivals to get the title party started in earnest.

MAY

BRENDAN Rodgers' side may have wrapped up the title, but their determination to preserve their high standards was evident in their first outing as seven-in-a-row champions, with Hearts put to the sword in the capital.

The Hoops were up against it in the early stages as Kyle Lafferty put the hosts in front, but they drew level though Dedryck Boyata's accurate header. In the second half, despite the difficult surface, the Hoops took control and inflicted the Tynecastle side's first home defeat of the season, courtesy of goals from Moussa Dembele and Scott Sinclair.

Next came the penultimate league meeting and also Celtic's penultimate home game which featured a much-changed side for the visit of Kilmarnock in the midweek clash.

The game finished goal-less with Celtic having the bulk of the pressure and among the youngsters taking part was 18-year-old Ewan Henderson making his debut from the bench.

Next up were Aberdeen and the 1-0 defeat couldn't take the shine off trophy presentation day and that paved the way for another trip to Hampden and seven-in-a-row was added to in some style. The 2-0 Scottish Cup final win over Motherwell delivered as an unprecedented Double Treble and thousands awaited at Paradise as the Eat-Sleep-Treble-Repeat open-top bus arrived with the Celts and the three trophies.

MAY FIXTURES (HOME FIXTURES IN BOLD)

6	SPFL	3-1	Hearts	(Boyata, Dembele, Sinclair)
9	**SPFL**	**0-0**	**Kilmarnock**	
13	**SPFL**	**0-1**	**Aberdeen**	
19	SC	2-0	Motherwell	(McGregor, Ntcham)

THE TOP 3

	P	W	D	L	F	A	GD	PTS
Celtic	**38**	**24**	**10**	**4**	**72**	**25**	**47**	**82**
Aberdeen	38	22	7	9	56	37	18	73
Rangers	38	21	7	10	76	50	26	70

INNERS 2018

IT'S ALL ACADEMIC

THE famed Celtic Youth Academy has the knack of producing some of the finest young footballers in Scotland.

Both the Hoops first team and the Scotland national side have been well-served by the likes of James Forrest, Kieran Tierney and Callum McGregor who have made their way through the ranks.

Hot on their heels are youngsters like Mikey Johnston, Anthony Ralston, Calvin Miller, Ewan Henderson and Jack Aitchison with many more joining the list.

So, Hail, Hail to the continuing success of the Celtic Youth Academy.

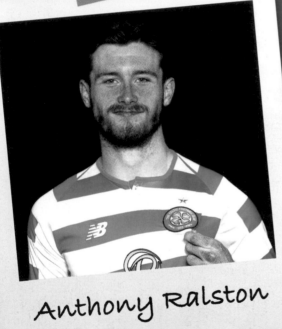

Anthony Ralston

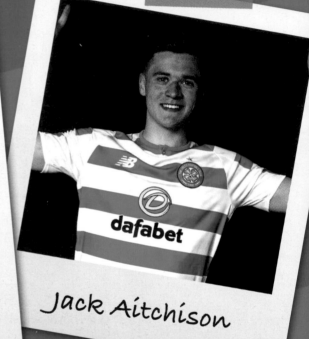

Jack Aitchison

Callum McGregor

Calvin Miller

Kieran Tierney

Mikey Johnston

James Forrest

Ewan Henderson

PLAYER PROFILES

SCOTT BROWN

Position: Midfielder
Squad Number: 8
D.O.B: 25/06/1985
Born: Dunfermline, Scotland
Height: 5'9"
Signed: 29/05/07
Debut: v Kilmarnock (h) 0-0, (SPL) 05/08/07
Previous Club: Hibernian

JAMES FORREST

Position: Midfielder
Squad Number: 49
D.O.B: 07/07/1991
Born: Prestwick, Scotland
Height: 5'9"
Signed: 01/07/09
Debut: v Motherwell (h) 4-0, (SPL) 01/05/10
Previous Club: Celtic Youth

CRAIG GORDON

Position: Goalkeeper
Squad Number: 1
D.O.B: 31/12/1982
Born: Edinburgh, Scotland
Height: 6'4"
Signed: 03/07/14
Debut: v St Johnstone (a) 3-0, (SPFL) 13/08/14
Previous Clubs: Sunderland, Hearts,
Cowdenbeath (loan)

MIKAEL LUSTIG

Position: Defender
Squad Number: 23
D.O.B: 13/12/1986
Born: Umea, Sweden
Height: 6'2"
Signed: 01/01/12
Debut: v Aberdeen (a) 1-1, (SPL) 03/03/12
Previous Clubs: Rosenborg, GIF Sundsvall,
Umea

TOM ROGIC

Position: Midfielder
Squad Number: 18
D.O.B: 16/12/1992
Born: Griffith, Australia
Height: 6'2"
Signed: 09/01/13
Debut: v Inverness Caley Thistle (a) 3-1, (SPL) 09/02/13
Previous Clubs: Central Coast Mariners, Belconnen United, ANU FC

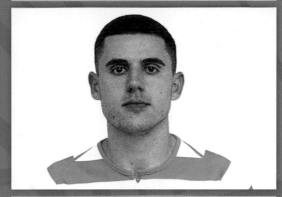

LEIGH GRIFFITHS

Position: Striker
Squad Number: 9
D.O.B: 20/08/1990
Born: Edinburgh, Scotland
Height: 5'9"
Signed: 31/01/14
Debut: v Aberdeen (a) 1-2, (Scottish Cup) 08/02/14
Previous Clubs: Wolverhampton Wanderers, Hibernian (loan), Dundee, Livingston

KIERAN TIERNEY

Position: Defender
Squad Number: 63
D.O.B: 05/06/1997
Born: Douglas, Isle of Man
Height: 6'0"
Debut: v Dundee (a) 2-1, (SPFL) 22/04/15
Previous Club: Celtic Youth

SCOTT SINCLAIR

Position: Midfielder
Squad Number: 11
D.O.B: 25/03/1989
Born: Bath, England
Height: 5'10"
Signed: 07/08/16
Debut: v Hearts (a) 2-1, (SPFL) 07/08/16
Previous Clubs: Aston Villa, Aston Villa (loan), West Bromwich Albion (loan), Manchester City, Swansea City, Wigan Athletic (loan), Birmingham City (loan), Crystal Palace (loan), Charlton Athletic (loan), Queens Park Rangers (loan), Plymouth Argyle (loan), Chelsea, Bristol Rovers

PLAYER PROFILES

DEDRYCK BOYATA

Position: Defender
Squad Number: 20
D.O.B: 28/11/1990
Born: Brussels, Belgium
Height: 6'2"
Signed: 02/06/15
Debut: v FC Stjarnan (h) 2-0, (UCL) 15/07/15
Previous Clubs: Manchester City, Bolton (loan), FC Twente (loan)

CALLUM McGREGOR

Position: Midfielder
Squad Number: 42
D.O.B: 14/06/1993
Born: Glasgow, Scotland
Height: 5'10"
Debut: v KR Reykjavik (a) 1-0, (UCL) 15/07/14
Previous Club: Celtic Youth, Notts County (loan)

YOUSSOUF MULUMBU

Position: Midfielder
Squad Number: 27
D.O.B: 25/01/1987
Born: Kinshasa, DR Congo
Height: 5'8"
Signed: 31/08/18
Previous Clubs: Kilmarnock, Norwich City, West Bromwich Albion, West Bromwich Albion (loan), Amiens SC (loan), Paris Saint-Germain

JOZO SIMUNOVIC

Position: Defender
Squad Number: 5
D.O.B: 04/08/1994
Born: Zagreb, Croatia
Height: 6'3"
Signed: 02/09/15
Debut: v Ajax (a) 2-2, (UEL) 17/09/15
Previous Club: Dinamo Zagreb

NIR BITTON

Position: Midfielder
Squad Number: 6
D.O.B: 30/10/1991
Born: Ashdod, Israel
Height: 6'5"
Signed: 30/08/13
Debut: v AC Milan (a) 0-2, (UCL) 18/09/13
Previous Club: FC Ashdod

DANIEL ARZANI

Position: Midfielder
Squad Number: 14
D.O.B: 04/01/1999
Born: Khorramabad, Iran
Height: 5'7"
Signed: 17/08/18
Debut: n/a
Previous Clubs: Manchester City, Melbourne City

DORUS DE VRIES

Position: Goalkeeper
Squad Number: 24
D.O.B: 29/12/1980
Born: Beverwijk, Netherlands
Height: 6'1"
Signed: 13/08/16
Debut: v Aberdeen (h) 4-1, (SPFL) 27/08/16
Previous Clubs: Nottingham Forest,
Wolverhampton Wanderers, Swansea City,
Dunfermline, ADO Deb Haag, Telstar

PLAYER PROFILES

SCOTT ALLAN

Position: Midfielder
Squad Number: 19
D.O.B: 28/11/1991
Born: Glasgow, Scotland
Height: 5'9"
Signed: 14/08/15
Debut: v Dundee United (a) 3-1, (SPFL) 22/08/15
Previous Clubs: Hibernian, Birmingham City (loan), Portsmouth (loan), MK Dons (loan), Portsmouth (loan), West Bromwich Albion, Forfar (loan), Dundee United

RYAN CHRISTIE

Position: Midfielder
Squad Number: 17
D.O.B: 22/02/1995
Born: Inverness, Scotland
Height: 5'10"
Signed: 01/09/15
Debut: v St Johnstone (h) 3-1, (SPFL) 23/01/16
Previous Club: Inverness Caledonian Thistle

FILIP BENKOVIC

Position: Defender
Squad Number: 32
D.O.B: 13/07/1997
Born: Zagreb, Croatia
Height: 6'4"
Signed: 31/08/18
Previous Clubs: Leicester City, Dinamo Zagreb

EBOUE KOUASSI

Position: Midfielder
Squad Number: 88
D.O.B: 13/12/1997
Born: Abidjan, Ivory Coast
Height: 6'1"
Signed: 12/01/17
Debut: v St Mirren (h) 4-1, (Scottish Cup) 05/03/17
Previous Clubs: Krasnodar

JONNY HAYES

Position: Midfielder
Squad Number: 15
D.O.B: 09/07/1987
Born: Dublin, Ireland
Height: 5'6"
Signed: 19/06/17
Debut: v Linfield (a) 2-0, (UCL) 14/08/17
Previous Clubs: Aberdeen, Inverness Caley Thistle, Cheltenham Town (loan), Northampton Town (loan), Leicester City, Milton Keynes Dons (loan), Forest Green Rovers (loan), Reading

ANTHONY RALSTON

Position: Defender
Squad Number: 56
D.O.B: 16/11/1998
Born: Bellshill, Scotland
Height: 5'11"
Debut: v St Johnstone (a) 1-2, (SPFL) 11/05/16
Previous Club: Celtic Youth

CALVIN MILLER

Position: Defender
Squad Number: 59
D.O.B: 09/01/1998
Born: Glasgow, Scotland
Height: 5'11"
Debut: v Partick Thistle (h) 1-0, (SPFL) 20/12/16
Previous Club: Celtic Youth

PLAYER PROFILES

MICHAEL JOHNSTON

Position: Striker
Squad Number: 73
D.O.B: 19/04/1999
Born: Glasgow, Scotland
Height: 5'10"
Debut: v St Johnstone (h) 4-1, (SPFL) 06/05/17
Previous Club: Celtic Youth

LEWIS MORGAN

Position: Midfielder
Squad Number: 16
D.O.B: 30/09/1996
Born: Greenock, Scotland
Height: 5'8"
Signed: 05/01/18
Debut: v Alashkert (a) 3-0, (UCL) 10/07/18
Previous Clubs: St Mirren

CRISTIAN GAMBOA

Position: Right-back
Squad Number: 12
D.O.B: 24/10/1989
Born: Liberia, Costa Rica
Height: 5'8"
Signed: 30/08/16
Debut: v Barcelona (a) 0-7, (UCL) 13/09/16
Previous Clubs: West Bromwich Albion,
Rosenborg, Copenhagen, Fredrikstad,
Municipal Liberia

ODSONNE EDOUARD

Position: Striker
Squad Number: 22
D.O.B: 16/01/1998
Born: Kourou, French Guiana
Height: 6'1"
Signed: 31/08/17
Debut: v Hamilton Accies (a) 4-1, (SPFL) 08/09/18
Previous Clubs: Toulouse (loan),
Paris Saint-Germain

KRISTOFFER AJER

Position: Defender
Squad Number: 35
D.O.B: 17/04/1998
Born: Raelingen, Norway
Height: 6'5"
Signed: 17/02/16
Debut: v Lincoln Red Imps (h) 3-0, (UCL) 20/07/16
Previous Club: IK Start

KUNDAI BENYU

Position: Midfielder
Squad Number: 26
D.O.B: 12/12/1997
Born: London, England
Height: 5'10"
Signed: 29/06/17
Debut: v Linfield (h) 4-0, (UCL) 19/08/17
Previous Clubs: Aldershot Town (loan),
Ipswich Town

JACK AITCHISON

Position: Striker
Squad Number: 76
D.O.B: 05/03/2000
Born: Fauldhouse, Scotland
Height: 5'8"
Debut: v Motherwell (h) 7-0, (SPFL) 15/05/16
Previous Club: Celtic Youth

PLAYER PROFILES

JACK HENDRY

Position: Defender
Squad Number: 4
D.O.B: 07/05/1995
Born: Glasgow, Scotland
Height: 6'2"
Signed: 31/01/18
Debut: v Kilmarnock (a) 0-1, (SPFL) 03/02/18
Previous Clubs: Dundee, Milton Keynes Dons (loan), Shrewsbury Town (loan), Wigan Athletic, Partick Thistle

SCOTT BAIN

Position: Goalkeeper
Squad Number: 29
D.O.B: 22/11/1991
Born: Edinburgh, Scotland
Height: 6'0"
Signed: 31/01/18
Debut: v Rangers (a) 3-2, (SPFL) 11/03/18
Previous Clubs: Hibernian (loan), Dundee, Alloa Athletic, Elgin City (loan), Aberdeen

EWAN HENDERSON

Position: Midfielder
Squad Number: 52
D.O.B: 27/03/2000
Born: Edinburgh, Scotland
Height: 5'9"
Signed: 01/08/17
Debut: v Kilmarnock (h) 0-0, (SPFL) 09/05/18
Previous Club: Celtic Youth

MARVIN COMPPER

Position: Defender
Squad Number: 33
D.O.B: 14/06/1985
Born: Tubingen, Germany
Height: 6'1"
Signed: 01/01/18
Debut: v Morton (h) 3-0, (Scottish Cup) 03/03/18
Previous Clubs: RB Leipzig, Fiorentina, 1899 Hoffenheim, Borussia Monchengladbach

EMILIO IZAGUIRRE

Position: Defender
Squad Number: 3
D.O.B: 10/05/1986
Born: Tegucigalpa, Honduras
Height: 5'10"
Signed: 18/08/10 and 10/08/18
First Debut: v Motherwell (a) 1-0, (SPL) 29/08/10
Previous Clubs: Al-Fayha, Celtic, Motagua

CONOR HAZARD

Position: Goalkeeper
Squad Number: 65
D.O.B: 05/03/1998
Born: Downpatrick, Northern Ireland
Height: 6'6"
Signed: 20/05/14
Previous Clubs: Celtic Youth

OLIVIER NTCHAM

Position: Midfielder
Squad Number: 21
D.O.B: 09/02/1996
Born: Longjumeau, France
Height: 5'9"
Signed: 12/07/17
Debut: v Linfield (h) 4-0, (UCL) 19/08/17
Previous Clubs: Genoa (loan), Manchester City

GETTING TO KNOW...
KRISTOFFER AJER № 35

What was the first CD album you bought or downloaded?

I remember buying some kind of '90s hits for kids, but it would probably be an album by the Norwegian band, A-ha, when I was much younger.

What sort of TV shows do you watch?

It would have to be 'Game of Thrones', which is on HBO. It's really good. I have seen it all. I started watching it last year and I saw everything within three or four months.

Which TV shows do you turn off?

I could stop watching 'Prison Break' after the first season, as the second, third and fourth ones weren't that good. It's always the same thing.

Name a stadium you haven't played in but would like to?

Anfield, just because of the atmosphere. They also sing 'You'll Never Walk Alone', not as good as Celtic Park, but it would be interesting to play there.

Do you have any pre-match superstitions?

I don't really have any but I must have a couple of hours' sleep in the middle of the day. That's the only thing that really sets me up for the game. There's nothing in particular as football means too much to me, I only enjoy getting ready for the game. I just look forward to the game so I am focused from the minute I wake up and really ready for the game.

Are there any other unusual superstitions you've come across?

Back in Norway there was a player that always showered at half-time. That was probably the strangest thing I've seen. Straight after the whistle he would rush into the shower and stood there singing to get ready for the second half.

What music do you listen to pre-match?

I listen to really calm stuff like Justin Bieber. Really slow, chilled out types of music. I don't like loud music with screaming at that point. Mainly boy bands and covers, that's really it.

How do you unwind after a match?

I prefer going back home. I enjoy just getting back to the apartment and relaxing. I'll maybe watch the TV and sometimes watch the game at another time by myself to learn more.

Is it harder to unwind after a bigger game, such as a UEFA Champions League match?

When you play in a bigger game it's more difficult to be able to relax when you go to bed. You start thinking about the game and when you start thinking about situations and what you could have done better or what you thought was good about the game, then you can never fall asleep. You can stay up thinking about the game for hours. After the Rosenborg match in 2017, I was awake for a few hours as I really enjoyed that game.

2017/18 Stats	Apps	Subs	Goals
League	23	1	0
League Cup	1	0	0
Scottish Cup	5	0	0
Europe	4	0	0
Total	33	1	0

COLOURING-IN

IT'S time to get out your crayons, ink markers or paints and bring this image of Celtic legend, Henrik Larsson at the Scott Brown testimonial to full vibrant green and white technicolour.

Scott Brown Testimonial Match
Celtic FC V Republic of Ireland XI
Celtic Park
20th May 2018

dafabet

MIX 'N' MATCH

See if you can match up the correct stats from last season to the player.

1. Scott Brown

2. Scott Sinclair

3. James Forrest

4. Callum McGregor

5. Kieran Tierney

6. Moussa Dembele

7. Tom Rogic

8. Scott Bain

9. Calvin Miller

10. Olivier Ntcham

A. Four Scottish Cup goals.

B. Seven league games.

C. Nine goals.

D. 56 appearances.

E. Three League Cup goals but only one start.

F. Only outfield player to start in all four League Cup matches.

G. Four appearances.

H. 18 goals.

I. 14 substitute appearances

J. Only player to score in all domestic and Euro competitions.

Answers on page 63.

LEAGUE CUP WIN No.17...
THE DOUBLE TREBLE WIN

PART ONE

CELTIC first won the League Cup in season 1956/57 with a 3-0 replay win over Partick Thistle and followed that up the following season with the historic 7-1 final victory over Rangers to record consecutive wins.

They didn't win it again, though, until season 1965/66, but that was part of no fewer than **FIVE** wins in a row in the competition and part of an amazing **FOURTEEN** consecutive finals in a row.

Since then there has been intermittent success, but the 2016/17 win was Brendan Rodgers' first trophy as a manager and Celtic's 100th top-level success as well as being part of the club's fourth treble.

The League Cup win of season 2017/18 saw Brendan Rodgers become the first manager to deliver the first four domestic trophies available to him and it was the crucial first part of the Double Treble.

It started with a 5-0 home win over Kilmarnock followed by a 4-0 win over Dundee at Dens Park before a 4-2 semi-final victory over Hibernian at Hampden Park.

It was then back to the National Stadium again for the final against Motherwell and a first-half James Forrest goal followed by a Moussa Dembele penalty after the turnaround sealed the 2-0 win.

The Double Treble was on...

WINNERS 2017

BETFRED CUP

FLAG DAY 2018

CELTIC FOOTB

CELTIC legend Danny McGrain had the honour of unfurling the club's seventh league flag in a row as the 2018/19 season kicked off with the opening game against Livingston.

The championship-winning flag was unfurled in front of a packed Paradise with, not only the SPFL trophy, but also the Scottish Cup and League Cup on show from the 2017/18 Double Treble campaign.

L CLUB 1888

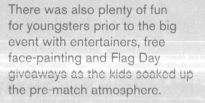

There was also plenty of fun
for youngsters prior to the big
event with entertainers, free
face-painting and Flag Day
giveaways as the kids soaked up
the pre-match atmosphere.

CHAMPIONSHIP WIN No.49...
THE DOUBLE TREBLE WIN

PART TWO

CELTIC first won the league title in season 1892/93 when they finished one point above Rangers and the following season they became the first side to solely retain the championship.

From 1904/05 until 1909/10, the Celts won six titles in a row which was a Scottish record until Jock Stein led the Hoops to an unforgettable nine-in-a-row between 1965/66 and 1973/74.

Since the turn of the Millennium, Celtic have won no fewer than **THIRTEEN** of the 18 title campaigns played.

The 2016/17 title, delivering another six-in-a-row, was won without losing a single game and the Hoops knew they would face a concerted challenge in taking the run to seven-in-a-row.

They faced that challenge head-on, though, with several landmark games over the course of the campaign but it all came to a head when Rangers visited Paradise on April 29.

Not only did the 5-0 win maintain Brendan Rodgers' 11-game unbeaten run against the Ibrox side, it delivered seven-in-a-row and the championship party got into full swing before the trophy was presented three games later on the final day of the campaign.

The Double Treble was still on...

DOT-TO-DOT

JOIN up all of the dots in this picture and see if you can identify what the Celtic image is.

Answer on page 63.

1 Brothers Liam and Ewan Henderson made one substitute appearance each in the league – but against which sides?

2 James Forrest scored his first Celtic hat-trick against which side?

3 Odsonne Edouard also scored his first Celtic hat-trick in a game against Motherwell – but who scored the other two Hoops goals in that game?

4 Which Celts scored in both the final and semi-final of the Scottish Cup?

5 Which Celt scored the first goal of the league campaign?

6 What was the score in Celtic's first League Cup game of the season?

7 How many home games did Celtic play in November?

8 The Hoops played three home games in a row in February – who were they against?

9 Who scored Celtic's goals in the away win over Anderlecht in the UEFA Champions League?

10 Jonny Hayes scored his only goal of the season against which side?

Answers on page 63.

GETTING TO KNOW...
KIERAN TIERNEY No.63

What was the first CD album you bought or downloaded?

It was probably Cascada or Akon or something like that. I was still into a bit of everything when I was younger. I can't remember for sure what phone I had it on, it was probably something like the Sony Ericsson Walkman phone.

What sort of TV shows do you watch?

I'd have to say 'Family Guy'. Every single night of my life I watch it.

Which TV shows do you turn off?

'Futurama'. I used to watch it but I was never able to get into it. I think it used to be on straight after 'The Simpsons' on Channel 4. 'The Simpsons' is far better.

Name a stadium you haven't played in but would like to.

I'm not really too fussed to be fair. I've never said I want to play in any stadium except Celtic Park for Celtic. You want to play in the biggest stadiums so maybe the Bernabeu.

Do you have any pre-match superstitions?

The night before, I always eat loads of chicken and pasta and fill myself up with that, but on the day I don't really do anything superstitious. I always put on my left sock and my left boot first, although if I don't do it, I don't take them off to put them on again.

Any unusual superstitions you've come across?

I know someone – I won't give away the name – who will only use the same toilet cubicle at Celtic Park before a game. There is always a bunch of us in the physio's room who do the quiz in the match programme, which passes a good 10 minutes.

What music do you listen to pre-match?

Just whatever's on in the changing room, which is a lot of chart music, like Hip-Hop and Rap. The guys have a playlist and every now and then it will be updated. For a few weeks in a row you will get the same songs but it's good music, I like it and it gets you up for a game.

How do you unwind after a match?

It depends. If we get beaten or draw, I will just stay in the house, have a wee bar of Dairy Milk and watch 'Family Guy', but if we win on a Saturday, then I'll maybe go out for a meal with my friends.

Is it harder to unwind after a bigger game, such as a UEFA Champions League match?

Definitely, as those games are usually at night so you aren't getting to sleep until three or four in the morning because you're still energised after the game. I'm sure most of the boys will say the same thing. Even if it's a game that isn't as big as a Champions League match, it's hard to unwind as there is so much going through your head and it takes you a while to fall asleep.

2017/18 Stats	Apps	Subs	Goals
League	30	2	3
League Cup	4	0	1
Scottish Cup	5	0	0
Europe	14	0	0
Total	53	2	4

SCOTTISH CUP WIN No.38...
THE DOUBLE TREBLE WIN

CELTIC first won the Scottish Cup in season 1891/92 when they defeated the then mighty Queen's Park 5-1 in the final.

The Hampden side had won nine previous Scottish Cups and had never lost a final until they met Celtic but would add a further one win for a total of 10 in all.

Celtic equalled that 10 with a 1-0 win over Hibernian in 1922/23 before overtaking it in a 2-1 win over Dundee in season 1924/25 and still lead the way in Scotland with a record 38 wins.

The 38th of those wins in the 2017/18 campaign kicked-off with a 5-0 win over Brechin City at Celtic Park before the Hoops welcomed Partick Thistle to the same venue and won 3-2.

Morton were next in the quarter-finals and the Greenock club were beaten 3-0, and the Celts found themselves facing Rangers in the semi-final.

The Ibrox club had no answer to Celtic's sharpness and power, and the Hoops motored to a 4-0 win and a place in the final against Motherwell.

The outcome was the same as the earlier League Cup final against the Fir Park side and the Celts were 2-0 up by the 25th minute and that's the way the scoreline stayed.

The Double Treble, the first ever in Scotland, was now a reality…

WINNERS 2018

EAT SLEEP TREBLE REPEAT

GET ON THE PARADISE BUS
The Double Treble comes home…

ANSWERS

Page 8 - Maze

Page 9 - Spot the Difference